BEING BULLIED IN THE WORK PLACE TO A SEASONED SCHOOL COUNSELOR

Barbara Brown

ISBN: 0692387927
ISBN 13: 9780692387924

INTRODUCTION

I wrote this book to share my experience of being bullied on my job. It will show how I was able to overcome being bullied for thirteen years. These were my last years to complete thirty years of service. Being bullied was a very difficult challenge. It could have made the difference of my having to settle for an early retirement. I was making a middle-class salary of one hundred thousand a year. Early retirement would have changed my salary to twenty thousand a year, a low income. For any of you who are being bullied on your job, I hope my story will inspire you to complete your career.

CHAPTER ONE

My supervisors used bullying to save the company money. Early retirement allows younger workers to replace a senior worker who makes a higher salary. These new workers would make up two of my salary.

Another issue that made it difficult for my supervisor was that I would report the bullying to the union. A younger worker would be more willing to comply with this behavior rather than report it. I also had tenure, which made it difficult for a supervisor to fire me. As a seasoned worker I had a lot of years under my belt. I was always willing to stand up during times when my supervisor would disrespect me by yelling at me in front of my coworkers. The yelling also was done in the presence of children I was working with. One of the students wrote me a letter and drew a picture of the supervisor yelling at me. Another student made a comment that my supervisor spoke to me "like a dog who don't listen."

There was no reason for the abuse, and I always kept a record of everything my supervisor did daily. I faxed a copy of this information to my union. This, in turn, led my supervisor to write tons of untrue accusations against me that were placed in my file. These letters stated that I was constantly late and that I did not support the students, parents, or my coworkers whom I worked with. The letters would always end with my supervisor threatening to take disciplinary action against me and terminate me and with a U rating. One thing I had on my side was that the parents and students were very supportive. The parents wrote reference letters on how they appreciated all the work I did for their children.

I became the scapegoat on the job and was isolated from coworkers who were afraid to lose their jobs. They would support the supervisor by giving her false information to support the untrue allegations. There was no trust between the supervisors and the workers. It was as though every person was concerned for his or her own selfish interest. Even the union representative avoided getting involved by allowing things to run its course. The union representative would agree with you in the absence of the supervisor but would side with the supervisor during the meetings. This made the representative's job less stressful and they were able to reap the benefits from the supervisor. The union representative was allowed to take extended weekends and holidays. At the end of the workday the supervisor had the final say, right or wrong. This is why I want my story to be told, for senior workers so they don't feel they are alone. As a school counselor I counseled children who bullied each other, but adults do it too—it's just that most people want to keep it a secret because it can have negative consequences.

My job became very stressful. I began to feel unproductive by not being able to do my best. Whenever I started a new program to support the students, other workers were given the credit.

I chose to work with children because I came from the same kind of background many of them did. I was raised in a foster home from age three. Being young themselves, my parents were not stable enough to raise six children. I left the foster care system and dropped out of school. At a young age I had three children myself. One was put up for adoption and another was killed by a young man who bullied him. One of the bully's teachers had warned the bully's family when he was young that he needed to get counseling for bullying students in his first-grade class.

I later went back to school and obtained three master's degrees, one in teaching and the other two in school counseling. I also completed a five-year degree in the ministry.

During my career I was written up in the daily newspaper for starting a mentor program in Brooklyn's challenged section. I have published three books guided by the Holy Spirit, *Short Love Poems by People Who Touched Our Lives, Sins Caused by the Absent Holy Spirit,* and my autobiography. I also obtained state and city licenses to become a certified teacher and school counselor.

I started an eyeglasses program where children were able to obtain a free eye exam and free eyeglasses from different optical businesses. Through this program students were able to score high scores on the city exams. The school was able to receive credit for going from a level C to a level A. The supervisor received grant money and different new electronic equipment. This equipment was given to staff and students. I still remained, however, with all my outdated materials and was never given credit for starting the program.

A few years after, all the funds had been spent. The school was investigated for using money inappropriately. As always everything became a secret. But when you are dishonest, things have a way of catching up. I would take children on the bus and train to the eye doctor. They really enjoyed meeting the optometrist who shared the type of work he did. The rest of his staff were very supportive as well. After their visit we would have lunch at their favorite fast-food restaurant. This was a change for them, to leave the neighborhood and low-income projects where they lived. It gave them a chance to see the nicer section of downtown Brooklyn, the up-and-coming middle- to upper-class lifestyle. Through their higher scores these students were accepted into a specialized program. This was another part of my job doing articulation. The specialized schools were not accepting of students who didn't come from their neighborhood.

I used my out-of-pocket money to pick up their glasses and pay for those children who did not have the money. I was an advocate asking different schools to accept our children. As time went on 90 percent of our children were accepted into top schools. My supervisor became very hostile toward me, stating the children should remain in their low-income poverty-ridden neighborhood. I continued to do all I could for the children to have a better future. Thank God to all those people—my foster parents, my good friends, and my school counselor—who gave me the opportunity to attend top colleges, New York University, Lehman College, and Brooklyn College.

I looked at the emotional support of the student as well as physical. If there was a need I was there. This went from doing hair to buying coats—it really didn't matter. A lot of parents could not afford some of the basic essentials of life for their children. My not having my own family gave me a lot of compassion for others.

I did not do the work to be recognized, only to support our future generation. I was blessed to have a great foster mom and dad who gave me positive guidance. The guidance they gave me was the importance of reading and education. I would need this later in my life. Now I realize the importance of education in terms of allowing me to obtain a good job with good retirement benefits. It really makes a difference in your salary whether or not you will have to work during your golden years.

I ran away from my second foster home at age fourteen. The city had taken me from my foster parents I'd known from age three. This change was very detrimental to me. Once you become aged out and the foster parents didn't adopt you, the agency became your guardian. They found a different foster home to place you in. I was separated from my other sibling and refused to go from place to place. I became very rebellious and went from being a 4.0 student to not caring. I saved my allowance to leave the foster home located in New

Jersey to live on the streets of the Bronx, New York. I was very naive and innocent, having been sheltered by my foster parents. I did manage to keep my dignity and respect by not turning to drugs and alcohol as other teenagers did.

During the early sixties the drug of choice was used by many young people. In order to support their habit they would turn to prostitution. The older men would introduce them to the drug. I saw a lot of young men and women destroy their lives. I knew in my heart this was a path I would never want to travel. I turned to older people, taking their advice on surviving the street life. I was blessed to meet people who were very supportive of me. I started to babysit for them when they went to work. They would allow me to stay at their home and eat food in return for my service. Then I became pregnant and was assigned to a case worker. Ms. H. was very instrumental in providing me with parenting skills. I also signed up to take classes to receive my GED. My son was born premature. This was very challenging for me, being a teenager without family support. This was a big challenge that would change my life forever. Having a social worker who was so supportive made me begin to see Ms. H. as my role model.

I knew one day in the future I would become a social worker. Once I received my GED I enrolled in a two-year associate program in psychology, and who did I have the pleasure of having as my college counselor but Ms. H. She had changed careers from social worker to counselor. She worked with me on getting the correct courses to graduate in two years. Once I received my associate degree I applied to NYU to their school of social work. Ms. H. wrote me a beautiful reference letter for the program. I received a scholarship from NYU and obtained my bachelor of social work in two years. Ms. H. was ready to retire and moved back to her hometown. She wished me the best, and she will never know how she changed my future. I wish there was a way to thank her for all she did. It's like I followed in her same footsteps. I did everything I could to pay her back by helping the children I worked with change their lives.

5

I began working in the school system in the early eighties. Those early years of my career were very exciting. I really looked forward to going to work. My first supervisor couldn't praise me enough. Being twenty-five I felt as though I was on top of the world. I was tall and slim with a Barbie-doll figure and a head full of hair. Life was really calling for me to make a change in the world.

Most of my students came from dysfunctional single-headed households. The majority of them did not have both parents. It was usually the mother, who was young with little experience. Their income came from welfare, and they had limited education. This took me to the place that I was born into before I was placed in foster care. My foster parents were married and lived in their own home. It was easy for me to understand the changes needed to help change the students' lives. It was as if I were giving back to all those people who had touched my life.

I poured my heart and soul into my job day after day. The students kind words and smiling faces showed so much hope for life. The students became very protective of me. Years later I transferred to another school. I ran into one of my parents and she wanted to thank me for working with her daughter in the first grade. Now she had grown into a young lady and was graduating from high school. They both invited me to attend the ceremony. Then the mother wanted to know if I had ever become a school counselor. I was able to tell her yes. By then I had changed my career from being a teacher to school counselor, a dream I'd had for years. And now I was sharing my dream with others, all from knowing Ms. H., my school counselor, who had inspired my life. Now I had been given the opportunity to help others the same way she helped me.

I used to love to decorate the classroom for holidays, and the children loved to pitch in. It was a pleasure to make their lives more productive.

Focusing on their education would prepare them for a better future. This would open up doors for them to become independent.

They would be able to choose a career to provide for themselves. A good education would allow them to have a brighter future, one in which they would not need to depend on people or the system for support.

I worked very hard during my career after school. Sometimes I would work two or three jobs while attending college full time. My career was doing so well, also my personal life. I became a Christian and put all my trust in God. It was like my life went from being labeled "the foster child" to "look at me now." I could remind people that God had brought me from nothing to something.

My, how time began to fly. I was getting older and no longer had the Barbie figure. Now that I was approaching my fifties I was experiencing middle-age changes, including my hair thinning.

The school system began to experience a lot of cutbacks. The mayor brought in younger teachers. Most of them came from other states. In return for their coming to the city they were given housing that the program paid for. They also were able to have their education paid for to obtain their master's degree. In order to receive these services the teaching students had to commit to working in the lower-income neighborhoods for three years. The majority of the schools took advantage of this because they could save money in their yearly budget. This was the cause of a lot of older workers being verbally abused by their immediate supervisor. The goal was to have the seasoned workers removed at any cost. There was little support from the union or willingness to get involved. Some senior workers became ATR, meaning they did not have a permanent school to call home. They would travel from school to school. This did not allow any supervisor to hire them because they were paid by city.

The teachers and other workers who had accumulated a lot of years remained in their permanent schools. The supervisors made them feel unworthy of all the work they'd accomplished. As for me, this was when my supervisor became very hostile and angry toward me. Through all my accomplishments I was constantly being isolated on the job. There was no opportunity for me to grow or be accepted. Many times I felt very left out. The new workers were given many chances to grow with the new changes in the school. They were allowed to attend workshops to enhance their expertise in the fields they worked in. I was forced by the supervisor to be in the lunchroom every day. My union would not cover me if I became injured. I had to monitor students who were in special classes for weeks to months at a time. A fight broke out and one of the students fell on top of me, causing my knee to twist to the side. This injury cost me a year of pain and suffering.

I had to go to physical therapy three times a week. I put in a claim to be signed by the supervisor, but she would not submit the papers. I was never compensated for the time, and the supervisor wrote me up to terminate my job. My doctor told her my condition could cause me to need an operation, but she continued to not allow me to stay off my feet. I would walk with a cane and lean on the wall in the lunchroom. She even moved me to a higher floor, which made it very difficult for me to go up and down. During the summer break my paycheck was cut thousands of dollars. I also was given a rating for the days I used for medical leave. For some unknown reason most of my doctor's notes were removed from my file. I was told I could not return to work unless the school's medical board cleared me. I spent the whole summer back and forth to the doctor who had to submit all my medical reports.

The medical department found the injury was true, and they informed my supervisor she had to remove the U rating. I was refunded all my money. This took a very long time, but I did eventually receive the money. After this dilemma I knew the supervisor would do anything to force me to retire by terminating me. She even told me one time, "I will make sure you don't receive your pension or social security." If this happened it would be very degrading to all I had worked for. I knew I had to do all I could and pray to make it until the end. My purpose of working with children had to be my priority. Even if

I had to be in the lunchroom I made the best of it. What had I ever done to the supervisor to make her so vile to me? I guess to this day I will never understand why she did the things she did. I was not looking for the status of needing to be accepted. My purpose was to be there for the children even though she disliked me for no reason. I was not there for whatever reason she felt she needed to torment me for.

I began to put all my energy into spending more time with the children. During lunch we would jump rope and have discussions on any problems they were having. During our group activities playing checkers and puzzles, I would take a lot of pictures. I started a picture scrapbook that of the students from pre-K to graduation. I used my time to give them a lifelong learning experience.

Another problem on the job was that I was not given a lunch period. If I took my lunch the supervisor would interrupt me by giving work to do. I complained to the union, but it never changed. The way I resolved this was to leave the building during my lunch.

The supervisor found out a student had been absent from school because the student was told by the assistant supervisor she was suspended. The supervisor threatened to give the assistant a U rating if she did not blame me, so she did.

I spent a lot of time writing to the union because I never had anything to say for what the supervisors wanted to do. The parent of the suspended student wrote a letter stating the *assistant supervisor* had told her daughter she was suspended. The assistant read the letter, then she told me I would throw her under the bus if I told the truth.

At the end of the school year I received a U rating. I requested a union hearing to explain my side but did not use the parent's letter. The supervisor requested I receive disciplinary action, be terminated, and get a U rating. She participated in the hearing via phone. During the session she threw me under the bus by making negative comments against me. Even though the union representative asked her why she hated me so, the supervisor lied and said, "That is not true."

I had all my documentation for all the work I'd done for the school, so the union said to the supervisor, "If it was not for Ms. Brown your school would not have done so well. It is all because of all the work Ms. Barbara Brown has done."

The union representative asked the supervisor if she remove the U rating, and the supervisor said no. At the end of the school term I received a U rating after thirty years of service. The assistant supervisor did not want to be responsible for what she'd done. To make matters worse she retired before the hearing. Her goal was not to retire with any blemishes on her record. I did get to retire, but the U rating would remain in my file during my retirement. I applied for a retirement certificate but was denied because of the U rating. The assistant was able to work, and she knew if she'd received a U she would not be able to. She later told me this after I retired, but thank God I don't need to work, just enjoy my retirement. The school went from an A school to a C after I left, and the supervisor was told she could never work in the school system again.

The last I heard whatever the supervisor had done—changing test scores and money not being unaccounted for—is still being investigated.

I think supervisors should respect the workers they supervise. We are not children and should all receive fair treatment. Most workers are looking for the American dream. They should not feel as they grow older they need to be pushed aside at the end of their careers. This time should be used as a contribution to future generations, and their years of wisdom, knowledge, and experiences should be recognized by society. I've seen workers come and go throughout my career. Some became sick from the stress of the job and had to go out on disability. A few even died from major illnesses before their retirement. The income they received for their illness would not compare to a full retirement check.

I hope my words of wisdom will let you know you are not alone, and I am praying for all of you to come retire in the Sunshine State.

Then you will know you have fulfilled your dream to just sit around and make your own schedule. There are no supervisors or coworkers to answer to. I pray the following words of spiritual wisdom will encourage senior workers to complete their full retirement. Some supervisors will not hesitate to throw you under the bus if it serves them in their retirement. Bullying can be used in any form, but the main reason it is used is to force people to leave their jobs. The ones who are not compassionate to older workers don't feel they will get older one day. They think they will be young always. They feel by tearing down other people who have worked so hard to get to where they are. They don't realize the way they treat people can affect others. This inappropriate behavior can be based on age, race, sexual orientation, education, job status, and different cultures, among other biases.

Some supervisors will not hesitate to throw you under the bus. There are three kinds of people: those who do bad things, those who sit around and do nothing, and the others who stand, alone, for what is right. Some people make you feel alone when you have done all you can for our children. Even when you reach out to them, they don't seem to care. Now you have to move forward to make a brighter future for yourself and others who care. Then you will be able to accept the fact that it's over, not knowing how the end will turn out, thanks be to God who saw us through. Scars remind us of where we've been, not where we are going. Everyone who doesn't come with you doesn't stay with you. Before I retired I attended my last union meeting. Many workers attended. One of my coworkers asked me whether I had done the right thing by attending the hearing. I was honored to say yes because others would not have had the courage or been afraid to stand up.

When those in authority mistreat people they should be held accountable. During the meeting the union shared with the staff that they needed to stand up against being treated unfairly. They were told they would receive all the support they needed. This would come from them uniting together. The union representative stated that

Ms. Barbara Brown had stood alone. She overloaded my fax machine, and I clapped for myself. Even though I'd stood alone, the time had finally come to see the staff sharing their experience of the mistreatment they had kept a secret. Now they could receive the equal treatment they all deserved. The abuse I faced so many years had been the same for them. I realize all I'd done was to inspire others to stand up for what was right and not accept anyone who didn't respect them. They also should be acknowledged for all their hard work during their difficult years.

It seems a lot of Christians and ordinary people are not showing the love to each other. They are not supporting each other for whatever reason. A lot of people who are struggling through life are left behind and have no one there when they need someone. Even when they reach out no one seems to understand. People seem to be caught up in their own selfishness in life. This makes it difficult to bring others in—or they lack the understanding of what each other need.

CONCLUSION

After thirty years of service I packed up my belongings. This was my last day at work. I was called to receive an award from my supervisor—this news was a big shock after all I'd been put through, but I had to have a forgiving heart. I received flowers and a plaque that read, "A state of mind living victoriously not bound by circumstance."

I proceeded back to my office to continue packing and thinking about the choices I'd made that were instrumental in preparing me for a good retirement. I am blessed not to have to work because I learned if you don't put any money away when you are young you will not have any when you get older. Like the saying "Don't play in the devil's backyard," you don't want to get old with no income. Now I can retire and enjoy all the fruits of my labor living in Florida. The gated community is located on a plantation of lakes and a golf course. It has its own transportation van and private clubhouse. They offer shows, movies, and exercise classes. My retirement car is a sports car, a 2014 Mercedes.

As I was looking forward on my last day in my office and everything was packed, I walked out my office door thinking like Jesus said on the cross, "It is finished." I turned around thinking of all I'd gone through. I said to myself that this would be my last time in this office. Then I walked to my car not wanting to say goodbye to anyone, just glad it was over. I am thankful to be able to share my career story to inspire others who feel they might not make it through. You will never know the reward of retirement until you have the experience. I hope reading about the tribulations and challenges I faced will give you the support you need to complete your retirement. Some of us are in denial. We only live for the moment. We are not concerned about what goes on around us. We continue to live from moment to moment. We are not concerned for the future. We are only satisfied today. We are blessed to be the best. Be thankful for those who are there for you and forgive those who are not. Let go and let God reveal what he has for the next chapter in your life. Learn to trust and depend on God, not in some people who take advantage during your weakness. They watch and do nothing, waiting to see you fall.

How we transfer from one chapter in our lives to another is how we got through. Each chapter determines our future in life. It will make or break us if we make poor or good decisions. These decisions can affect others in a positive or negative way. Others may follow in our footsteps, which can influence them for life. Influences may come from friends, family, or relationships. It is best to plan life prayerfully and carefully for life-changing events. If we do not we will not be prepared to share the good things in life. How can I be loved when I was never loved? How can I appreciate a friend when I never learned to be a friend? How can I trust when my trust was taken away? Some people who grow up being disappointed tend to disappoint others who come into their lives.

Why are we here? Life is living to support others and ourselves. Our lives don't belong to us; only to God who made us do we belong. Don't worry about people from your past. There is a reason they didn't make it into your future. People can cause you to wander. Be transformed by the renewing of your mind. Stop letting people talk you out of what God has called you to be and have. When you ask the approval of your critics, you give them the power. We have a right to be happy. Be around people who add positive things to your life or God will have someone do it for you. People should not be intimidated by your success. You should be accepted, not tortured by the wrong people. God does not give us the power of fear but of a sound mind. At the end everyone shows who they really are. Whatever end that could be.

RETIREMENT

Receive what God has for your life.

Enjoy rest and do nothing for all the fruits of your labor.

Trust in God to see you through everything; you have to surrender all.

Interesting things will come to you from God you couldn't imagine.

Receive what God wants for your life.

Enjoy all the things God gives to sustain us through the good and bad times.

Means to a new chapter of our lives.

Entertain yourself with all the things you were not able to do and say what you were not able to say.

Now you don't need others' approval as you did in the past—you only need God's.

Sometimes he allows us to go through the lowest point in our lives so we can learn to lean on and trust him.

Never give up because we have to know God has brought us through this far and he will never leave us or forsake us.

This destroys future good relationships. When you teach some-one to think, to be able to make good choices, you teach them to survive a long, prosperous life. This is a time to look ahead after mov-ing on forward, when you have done all you can by standing up to the truth. Even if it means others might not understand and you have to deal with your pain, still stand for the truth in life's disappointments. People don't always see the truth.

Teach the next generation how they should be prepared to enjoy all the fruits of their labor by God's unchanging hand—he never changes through the storm or through the rain or through our ups and downs. If our hearts are right God will always see us through because he holds our future.

All, and say thank you, Jesus! You have been so good to me. Then you can be free to love God fully. Praise him. Lift him up. And he can become the only one in each and every moment of your life. This is when you know you have surrendered all! Because you owe it all to him, and he gets all the glory—no one else. And now you can feel free to praise him no matter where you are or where you are going. Then you can share with the world your testimony of God's goodness. Now you can freely sing the song "Take Me to the King" because God holds our destiny from beginning to end, and you will be rewarded for all your hard work.

ECCLESIASTES 3:1

"To Everything there is a season, and a time to every purpose under the heaven. 2: A time to be born and a time to die, a time to plant and a time to pluck up that which is planted. 3: A time to kill and a time to heal, a time to break down and a time to build up. 4: A time to weep and a time to laugh, a time to mourn and a time to dance. 5: A time to cast away stones and a time to gather stones together, a time to embrace and a time to refrain from embracing. 6: A time to get and a time to lose, a time to keep, and a time to cast away. 7: A time to read, and a time to sew, a time to keep silence and a time to speak. 8: A time to love, and a time to hate, a time of war and a time of peace. 9: What profit hath he that worketh in that wherein he laboureth. 13: And also that every man should eat and drink and enjoy the good of all his labour, it is the gift of God. 14: I know that whatsoever God doeth it shall be forever nothing can be put to it, nor anything taken from it: and God doeth it that men should fear him. 17: I said in mine heart God shall judge the righteous and the wicked for there is a time there for every purpose and for every good works.

God bless all of
you in good health
and a long life to
enjoy your retirement. Amen